Biblical
Studies
Today

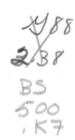

A GUIDE TO CURRENT
ISSUES AND TRENDS

EDGAR KRENTZ

Concordia Publishing House

St. Louis, Mo.

Concordia Publishing House, St. Louis, Missouri
Concordia Publishing House Ltd., London, E. C. 1
© 1966 by Concordia Publishing House

Library of Congress Catalog Card No. 66-29455

MANUFACTURED IN THE UNITED STATES OF AMERICA

Biblical Monographs ✷ ✷

Concordia Biblical Monographs are designed to acquaint readers with current developments in Biblical interpretation. Some of the authors merely report positions of Biblical scholars on specific issues without evaluating them. Others present a constructive essay on a subject of Biblical theology.

In *Biblical Studies Today* Edgar Krentz outlines the positions of leading scholars on the use of research methods and on issues in current debate.

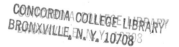

Contents

Introductory Chapter

Biblical studies today stand in striking contrast to Biblical studies in 1920. What were then regarded as assured results are today called into question. The assumptions underlying methods have changed. Methods themselves have been developed and refined. While this essay has as its primary object the description of current issues and problems in Biblical scholarship, some background is necessary to understand what is being done today.

In the first place, old style liberal theology has largely disappeared since the First World War. Historical positivism, individualism, and a rather naively optimistic (at least to us) anthropology gave way to dialectical theology and a more pessimistic spirit. The change was begun by Karl Barth's *Commentary on Romans* (1919), a strong call for a return to theological exegesis. At the same time "Word of God" or "kerygma" theology arose in the Bultmann school. These both influenced methodology and the type of questions addressed to the Scriptures.

Concurrently there was also a development in methodological techniques. The failure of 19th century historical methods to get back to the historical Jesus had a theological impasse. Historical methodology had not been able to recover the Jesus upon whom the historical religion, Christianity, was based. This led on the one hand to a skepticism over against historical methods and on the other hand to a search for techniques to take the historian behind the documents to their preliterary stage.

The generation between the wars also saw another change. The Enlightenment had begun the domination of Biblical scholarship by the Germans. Today a much more ecumenical and international scholarship is at work on the Scriptures. The days are now past when German Protestant professors work in a linguistic and confessional island. One reason is that the Roman Catholic Church has since 1900 produced Biblical scholars of the first water, especially in the French and German language areas. No responsible scholar today can overlook the monographs, journals, and commentaries produced by Roman scholars. Moreover, Anglo-Saxon and Scandinavian contributions have also succeeded in raising some of the questions that are being discussed today.

These pages were written on a sabbatical leave in Germany in the spring of 1964. Their specific weight and emphases would probably have been different, had they been written in America. More attention would probably have been given to hermeneutics.

The aim of this essay is to describe in simple fashion the present state of Biblical studies. While the issues of today cannot be understood apart from the history that produced them, limitations of space make it impossible to recount that history here. Interested readers will find guidelines for reading in the bibliographies at the end of each chapter. Nor will this report be complete. It must content itself with discussing some issues that are of central concern today. The presentation is intended to be an introduction to the reader who has little knowledge of the methods and concerns of Biblical scholarship. For that reason it is descriptive rather than argumentative. It is hoped that the reader will gain some idea of the complexity of the problems that are the bread and butter of the Biblical scholar.

The Biblical scholar works in many different areas of research. A knowledge of the Biblical languages (Hebrew, Aramaic, and Greek) is a necessary prerequisite for his work. Familiarity with the methods of linguistic and grammatical research is presupposed. Paleography (the reading of ancient scripts and manuscripts) and textual criticism (the evaluation of different manuscripts), a knowledge of contemporary literature (Babylonian, Egyptian, Ugaritic, Canaanite, Greek, Latin, etc.), art, and history are all part of the necessary intellectual background. The Old Testament scholar must have a firm grasp of the archaeology and comparative religion of the ancient Near East. The New Testament scholar must be at home, to some degree, in intertestamental literature and history and in Hellenistic and Rabbinic Judaism. In Biblical introduction he deals with the historical questions about the origin and authorship of Biblical books. Closely related to introduction is the history of the canon, that is, the collection of the individual books into the Bible in the history of Israel and the church. The interpretation of the text of the various books lies at the heart of all Biblical scholarship. Interpretation raises the problem of hermeneutics, that is, of the proper method of understanding a Biblical text and the presuppositions one should have in approaching a book of the Bible. The writing of Biblical history (of the Old or the New Testament) demands a grasp of all the aforementioned disciplines. All come together in the writing of the theology of the Old or New Testament. Finally, the history of interpretation is also of importance as a guide and corrective to one's own work.

A report on all these areas of research would result in a large book. The topics treated in this short essay were determined by the writer's competence and their present importance. Specialists will have no trouble in finding gaps, over-simplifications, and distortions in these pages caused by compression and the writer's limitations. He has attempted to represent and not to caricature positions of radically different schools of thought. That the New Testament receives more attention than the Old is a measure of the writer's interest. If the general reader will have received some insight into the interpreter's workshop, methods, and problems, then the booklet will have done what it sets out to do.

BIBLIOGRAPHY

General Works and Works of History

Fuller, Reginald H. *The New Testament in Current Study.* New York: Charles Scribner's Sons, c 1962.

Hahn, H. F. *The Old Testament in Modern Research.* Philadelphia: The Muhlenberg Press, 1954.

Hunter, Archibald M. *Interpreting the New Testament, 1900—1950.* Philadelphia: Westminster Press, 1951.

Krauss, Hans Joachim. *Geschichte der historisch-kritischen Erforschung des Alten Testaments von der Reformation bis zur Gegenwart.* Neukirchen Kreis Moers: Verlag der buchhandlung des Erziehungsvereins, 1956.

Kümmel, Werner Georg. *Das Neue Testament: Geschichte der Erforschung seiner Probleme.* Freiburg: Verlag Karl Alber, 1958.

Marty, Martin E., ed. *New Directions in Biblical Thought.* New York: Association Press, 1960.

Neill, Stephen. *The Interpretation of the New Testament, 1861—1961.* Fair Lawn, N. J.: Oxford University Press, 1964.

Robinson, James M. "Basic Shifts in German Theology," *Interpretation,* XVI (1962), 76 ff.

Schnackenburg, Rudolf. *Neutestamentliche Theologie. Der Stand der Forschung*. München: Kösel Verlag, c 1963. An earlier, shorter version in English, *New Testament Theology Today*. New York: Herder and Herder, 1963.

One can also consult with profit the relevant articles in two recent reference works:

The Interpreter's Dictionary of the Bible. New York: Abingdon, 1963.

Die Religion in der Geschichte und Gegenwart. 3 Aufl. Tübingen: J. C. B. Mohr, 1957—62.

2

The Historical Method

Scholars generally think of the Bible as a small library whose books span millenia in their content and origins. Most of the books were written for specific, often *ad hoc* purposes in definite historical situations. The message of each work is tied to this historically conditioned position. To understand that message today one must know the factors that made the author write and that influenced his literary formulation. In this respect the Bible is not at all unique but like every other work of literature. There is, in general, a noteworthy consensus among Biblical scholars of varied confessional backgrounds and theological positions that the historical critical method is today indispensable for understanding and interpreting the Scriptures. These scholars maintain that it is not a mark of outstanding piety or religious

13

awe before the Scriptures to refuse to use historical criticism. Indeed, according to those who advocate it, "responsible interpretation of the Scriptures in the service of the public proclamation of the Gospel in the sense of Augsburg Confession XIV *(publice docere)*" cannot be carried on if historical work is ignored. (Kurt Frör)

A. HISTORICAL BACKGROUND

Historical critical scholarship seeks to put the contents of the Bible into an historical order and framework. It determines as precisely as possible what a text meant for a man of its time, what the history of the material was before it was put into writing, and what opposing position, if any, a Biblical author was combatting. This is criticism's historical function. The method earns the name critical because it constantly asks about the bias and trustworthiness of the text and its author. Critics are concerned that they use the tools of the best current literary and historical research. In its techniques, i. e., as a method, critical scholarship is nonreligious and secular.

This approach to the Scriptures is the result of a development that began with the Enlightenment in the 17th century and led in the 19th century to historical positivism (=historicism) and liberal theology. Historicism can be characterized by the three words change, progress, and personality. It involved a radical relativizing of all historical traditions together with a concentration on ethics. Man is in a process of development that can be traced by the investigation of the facts of history. On the one side, therefore, historical positivism laid great stress upon the documents of history. Most of the great document collections date from its time. In studying these documents the 19th century sought objectivity, an approach without any dogmatic precommitment or bias. The ideal historian claimed only logic and the validity of the cause and effect relationship as necessary presuppositions.

It is still this method that many critics identify as *the* historical critical method. But time has changed historical methodology too, as it changes most everything. Two men and their followers, in particular, have contributed to this change in theological circles. (Philosophers too have made contributions, e. g. R. G. Collingwood, K. Löwith, and H. G. Gadamer.) Karl Barth and Rudolf Bultmann ushered in a radical change of climate in theology and initiated a hermeneutical discussion that is still in progress. Both questioned that exegesis, even if it used the historical critical method, could be objective.

Karl Barth has called for a "theological exegesis" in both his *Commentary on Romans* and in his *Church Dogmatics*, I. Barth's starting point was the analogy to Christology that exists in the Scriptures. As God was active in the man Jesus, so the Word of God meets us in the words of men: the prophets and apostles. We must read the Bible historically in order to meet the Word of God. But the historical method must be conditioned by its object. It must presuppose that it will hear God's Word. It seeks only one truth, and so interpretation is not a two stage (1) profane, (2) sacred hearing of the Word. Hermann Diem has carried this type of inquiry forward.

Rudolf Bultmann combines historical methodology with existential philosophy's understanding of history in order to escape the impasse of historicism. He wishes the Scriptures to speak powerfully in the present. On the one hand the Scriptures are, like any other book, the object of historical inquiry, which seeks the facts. But no absolute meaning is to be found in the facts. Meaning is to be found only as man personally confronts history and finds meaning for his own existence (existential interpretations). Only as man is not subjected to a strange world view is he set free to believe. It is this self-understanding that determines the work of interpretation, for interpretation must give free play for faith, God's creation. It is in this context that Bultmann's demythologizing must be placed. (The demythologizing debate is too long and involved to be reviewed here. Interested readers are referred to the voluminous literature on the subject.)

B. THE TECHNIQUES USED IN HISTORICAL CRITICAL METHODOLOGY

The first step in the study of an ancient text is the establishment of the text. *Textual criticism* is based on an evaluation of the available manuscripts and early translations in the light of the "laws" of textual transmission and a knowledge of the author's style and literary form. For the NT there is a rich store of available manuscript evidence. The OT has far fewer manuscripts to consult and, apart from the Qumran texts, these are a millenium or more later than the autographs. Because of the systematic destruction of variant OT texts by the Massoretes, the OT scholar is often forced to emend (correct) the Hebrew text on the basis of early translations (e. g. Greek or Syriac) or, in the case of very corrupt and unintelligible passages, to conjecture what it might have been, i. e. to make an educated guess.

When the text is established, then *literary* and *historical criticism* follow. While these may be conceptually separated, in practice they work hand in hand. With the aid of grammatical and philological analysis of the text, literary criticism determines an author's purpose in writing, the literary form used, the integrity and authenticity of a work, and its sources. Historical criticism is concerned with the historical context in which the work is written and also the prehistory of the work. *Form criticism,* a branch of both literary and historical criticism, seeks to recover the original form of a narrative by stripping off supposedly later additions (especially in the Gospels) and seeks to determine the original *Sitz im Leben* (sermon, liturgy, catechesis, etc.) of the form. It is also used in the study of the historical books of the OT, the Psalter, prophetic writings, Acts, NT epistles, and Revelation. *Tradition history* is the counterpart to form criticism; it traces the history of the preliterary form in its relation to places, cult, etc. Historical criticism also correlates what is learned in the Scriptures with the results of archaeology and what is known of the literary, religious, social, legal, and political life of the contemporaneous world. Finally, using the history of religions, the critic determines what was taken over from the environment by Biblical authors, how it was molded in Biblical thought, and thereby seeks to isolate the distinctive and unique elements in the Biblical authors. (It should perhaps be added that this comparison is also made between different authors in the Scriptures themselves.) These techniques are "secular and dangerous" (Erich Dinkler) and common to all literary and historical criticism. In that sense the method of Biblical research is no different from that of historical research in general. It shares means, method (logic, hypotheses, and subjective understanding), and objective with all historical research.

Theological criticism follows (my translation of the German *Sachkritik*). There is no precise agreement as to what this means. Some argue that the center of NT theology must be applied to judge all theological positions in the NT. Some find this center in Luther's "was Christum treibet" or in the Pauline doctrine of justification. Others see here the responsibility of deciding whether a given theological statement or doctrine measures up to the situation which called it forth, or whether the proclamation is too weak, inadequately formulated, or abbreviated to do its intended task. Theological criticism seeks to pass judgment on the variety of theological conceptions in the canon.

C. THE PRESUPPOSITIONS INVOLVED

Nineteenth-century historicism had attempted to reach objective historical judgments. Present-day Biblical criticism no longer speaks of objectivity in this sense. Indeed, it expresses its presuppositions and thereby makes clear its stand over against historical positivism. Some of these presuppositions are:

1. The Bible is an ancient book; it therefore requires interpretation not only because it is written in languages that are no longer readily understandable but also because its conceptual world is different from ours. Moreover, Christianity is a religion founded on historical happenings. Since the development of the historical method has taken place, not to use the method would betray the Gospel, for that would be to admit that the Bible cannot stand the test of historical investigation. Rather one must seek to use the method consistently and correctly.

2. Objectivity is impossible. Each interpreter comes out of a tradition and a personal history that in part determines his own method of seeking truth, meaning, and salvation. The historical critic is therefore not without presuppositions (Voraussetzungslos),

but is without preconceived judgments (Vorurteils-los). Here, according to contemporary critics, the middle of the 20th century sharply separates itself from classical liberal theology. Meaning in history is not found in the bare facts (which are always ambiguous) but in an understanding confrontation with the interpretation of the facts that leads one to find meaning in the present and to make a personal decision. For example, historical research can establish the fact that Jesus died under Pontius Pilate by crucifixion. It cannot establish that he died *pro me*. This is part of the interpretation of the facts.

3. The historian's "preunderstanding" is determined by the object of research, in this case the Bible itself. Since it claims to be a witness to God's activity in history, the historical critic seeks to hear that witness. He presupposes that God's Word is before the Scriptures, is witnessed to in the Scriptures, but is not identical with the Scriptures. Erich Dinkler has put it: "That the Bible and the Word of God, and that the Holy Scriptures and the kerygma are not identical is a presupposition of Biblical criticism." It should be noted here that Word of God in Dinkler's mind does not equal everything that God says, but the kerygma (i. e. the proclamation of forgiveness and grace that comes through God's gracious acts in history and that demands decision, i. e. the Gospel). Biblical criticism seeks to make this kerygma clear and articulate in the modern world. Its practitioners claim that the use of the critical method

is not the result of a loss of awe before the Word of God, nor do those who avoid its use show a greater piety than its practitioners. Whereas 19th-century criticism had placed the Word of God on a level with the words of men, present-day critics claim to practice their criticism out of awe before the Gospel.

4. Historical critics claim to be the heirs of Jesus, Paul, and the Reformation precisely in their critical stance. Historical critics recognize that the concept of history that originated with the Enlightenment was new. Nevertheless the critics find a precedent for their work in Jesus' setting of His own words ("I say unto you . . .") against the Mosaic law in Matt. 5 and in Paul's distinction of letter and spirit in 2 Cor. 3. So too Luther is claimed as a spiritual ancestor in his description of apostolicity as being that which "urges Christ" and in using this canon to relegate James, Revelation, and other NT books to a secondary place at the end of his NT translation of 1523. Similarly they cite his expression in his *Theses on Faith* of 1535: "If our adversaries urge Scripture against Christ, we will urge Christ against the Scripture." As for Luther, so for many German critics the doctrine of justification is the critical touchstone which allows the radical use of the critical method (Ernst Käsemann) and justifies the application of theological criticism against James, 2 Peter, the Pastorals, and Luke. The Law/Gospel antithesis of Lutheran theology makes critical Biblical study for them a necessary corollary of the Reformation's

sola fide. For history can neither establish nor destroy faith. Faith is the result of the proclamation of the Gospel and the work of the Holy Spirit. Historical critics therefore seek to set the Gospel into sharper focus and clarity.

D. RESULTS CLAIMED

Proponents of historical criticism claim certain results for their work. These results justify the use of the method in their opinion.

1. Historical criticism when properly carried on contains within itself the means for self-correction. Granted that its results are likely to mirror the historical views of its day, its concern with its object, the Bible, will still correct basically false trends. An example of this is the destruction of the older liberal theology with its optimistic view of man and its positivistic, evolutionary view of history. It was also critical theology which showed from the Scriptures the inadequacy of the liberal view of man and history.

2. Historical critical theology takes the credit for having discovered (or rather rediscovered) the importance of NT eschatology. Orthodox systematics had relegated eschatology to the end of dogmatics, to the *locus de novissimis.* Liberal theology and the Social Gospel in America reduced Jesus to an ethical teacher and model. It was the history of religions school and the practitioners of form criticism who restored eschatology to the center of the message of Jesus (Johannes Weiss, Albert Schweitzer, etc.). Today some of Rudolf Bultmann's pupils are finding

the same eschatological apocalyptic background for the epistles of Paul.

3. The historical critical method claims to have recovered for the church the urgency which characterized NT preaching. Practitioners insist that there is no gulf between historical criticism and the pulpit — indeed that responsible preaching must make use of the method.

4. Finally, historical critical students claim to have freed the church from a false concept of truth, i. e. from the belief that only that is true which can be demonstrated critically and historically (Edward Schweizer). Fear of the historical critical method, they would say, arises out of the same sort of historical positivism (the view that reality is only to be predicated of that which is verifiable by modern historical methods of research) that characterized 19th-century liberalism. But if faith does not have to rest upon historically verifiable facts, then truth exists which does not depend upon historical proof, indeed may even exist in spite of it. The resurrection of Christ would be the primary example. It cannot be proved historically, according to the canons of modern historiography; it can only be preached, witnessed, and believed.

BIBLIOGRAPHY

Methodology

Bultmann, Rudolf. "Is Exegesis Without Presupposition Possible?" *Existence and Faith,* tr. Shubert Ogden. New York: Meridian, 1960. Pp. 289—96.

Biblical Studies Today

Cullmann, Oscar. "The Necessity and Function of Higher Criticism," *The Early Church: Studies in Early Christian History and Theology*. Ed. A. J. B. Higgins. Philadelphia: Westminster Press, 1956. Pp. 3—16.

Diem, Hermann. *Was heisst Schriftgemäss?* Neukirchen Kreis Moers: Verlag der Buchhandlung des Erziehungvereins, 1958.

Ebeling, Gerhard. "The New Heremeneutic and the Early Luther," *Theology Today*, XXI (1964—65), 34—46.

———. "The Significance of the Critical Historical Method for Church and Theology in Protestantism," *Word and Faith*. Tr. James W. Leitch. Philadelphia: Fortress Press, 1963. Pp. 17—61.

Frör, Kurt. *Biblische Hermeneutik: Zur Schriftauslegung in Predigt und Unterricht*. München: Chr. Kaiser Verlag, 1961. Pp. 11—85.

Knox, John. *Criticism and Faith*. New York: Abingdon-Cokesbury, 1952.

Preus, Robert. "Schriftautorität, Offenbarungsverständnis und historische Methode," *Lutherischer Rundblick*, XII (1964), 2—12.

Robinson, James M., and John B. Cobb, Jr. *The New Hermeneutic*. New York: Harper & Row, 1964.

Schweizer, Eduard. "Die historisch-kritische Bibelwissenschaft und die Verkündigungsaufgabe der Kirche," *Evangelische Theologie*, XXIII (1963), 31—42. Reprinted in *Neotestamentica*. Zürich/Stuttgart: Zwingli Verlag, c. 1963. Pp. 136—49.

3

Source and Form Criticism

Biblical scholarship is historical scholarship. As such it uses the methods of historical research which set documents into their historical time and framework. But historical criticism also asks about the truth and factuality of events. It wishes to know what happened. When more than one account is present (as in the four Gospels) or when apparently contradictory accounts are present (was Bethel given its name on Jacob's way to Mesopotamia as in Gen. 28 or on his return as in Gen. 35?), then accounts and documents must be evaluated.

Some documents are primary sources, i. e. written by participants or eyewitneses. Such, for example, is Paul's account of the Jerusalem Council in Gal. 2. (Some scholars, of course, would say this is the visit of Paul recorded in Acts 11:30.) Other works

are written by people who depend for their information on other documents or people (cf. Luke 1:1-4).
Acts 15 is in this perspective a secondary source for
the Jerusalem Council, whether it is or is not regarded as a report of the same event described in
Gal. 2. The terms primary and secondary are not
necessarily value judgments on documents. A secondary report may be taken from a better observer than
the author of a primary account. Moreover, the purpose and form of a document must be observed.
Pilate's account of Jesus' trial included in his official
papers would, if we had it, read quite differently
from any of the Gospel accounts — and might yet
be entirely accurate. Evaluation is thus necessary
in handling documents.

When more than one account is available, the
critical historian looks for identity, similarity, variation, discrepancy, and outright contradiction and
from them reconstructs the event that could lead
to such reports. In the case of secondary documents
he attempts to identify and evaluate the sources
used in them by separating the sources from the
author's editorial work on them. Depending upon
the documents, different techniques have been used.

A. SOURCE ANALYSIS

Present-day scholars have inherited two major
reconstructions of sources in the Biblical texts that
are generally accepted as working hypotheses, although current scholarship tries to make them more
precise. These can only be sketched here in the bar-

est outline. No scholar would probably agree completely with the outline as presented here. In each case the theory arose out of a desire to get to the oldest account in the Scriptures where more than one was present.

1. *The Pentateuch*

Old Testament students inherit the analysis of the Pentateuchal sources classically formulated by Julius Wellhausen in the 19th century. This theory proposes four sources. The two earliest are named J (named for its use of Jahweh as name for God) and E (named for its use of Elohim for God). Each has its own peculiarities. J has a brilliant style, uses many anthropomorphisms of God, is concerned with clan history and national history, gives the Decalog in the form quoted in Ex. 34:12-26, and emphasizes Abraham and Judah. J likely has Southern origin in the time of David (i. e. ninth century B. C.). E is concerned more with Jacob and the history of Reuben and Joseph, tells the story of the revelation of the name Jahweh to Moses, uses the name Horeb rather than Sinai for God's holy mountain, presupposes a fixed agricultural community (cf. "Book of the Covenant," Ex. 20:22—23:33), and likely originated in the North in the eighth century B. C. Both sources drew on earlier material, especially in the formulation of legal codes.

In the seventh century B. C., according to this critical source theory, the Book of Deuteronomy was composed. Discovered in the temple in the time of Josiah, D led to a great reform in Israel. In relatively simple literary style D calls for a pure cult without contamination by Canaanite practices. Whereas the earlier documents still knew of diversified cultic centers, here Jerusalem is emphasized. The emphasis on centralization was based on the desire to exercise control over the cult of Israel. The Books of Samuel and Kings, possibly also Joshua and Judges, were written under the influence of the Deuteronomic view of history. All were based on this urge for centralization.

The last source, called P for priestly, is theologically related to Ezekiel and according to the theory was likely composed in Babylon in the same period. It too used much older material to attempt a still more stringent regulation of Hebrew cult through a graded priesthood. J and E had described individual sacrifice, D regarded all Levites as priests, but P concentrated on the Aaronites (the Levites become "assistants"). The exact number and date of the editors who combined these sources into our present Pentateuch is not known. It is relatively certain, according to the critics, that the redaction was completed by 400 B. C. Therefore, while the source analysis of the Pentateuch set out to find the old, Mosaic basis of the Pentateuch, it ended up with a series of documents and editorial revisions extending from the ninth to the fourth centuries before Christ. The answer was no solution of the problem.

2. *The Synoptic Problem*

The problem of sources was raised in the synoptic gospels by two main facts. (1) The same material was not to be found in the same order in all Gospels (to say nothing of variation in detail). (2) Matthew and Luke had a significant amount of material in common that was not in Mark and each had a stock of peculiar material. Differences of order and detail raised the problems of chronological accuracy and of factual precision. Did the cleansing of the temple take place on Palm Sunday (Matt. 21:12-17) or on Monday of Holy Week (Mark 11:12-19)? Did the voice from heaven at Jesus' baptism say "This is . . ." (Matt. 3:17) or "You are . . . (Mark 1:11= Luke 3:22)? Is the order of the temptations correct in Luke or in Matthew? Did the would-be disciples present themselves to Jesus before or after Peter's confession at Caesarea Philippi (cf. Matt. 8:18-22 and Luke 9:57-62)? The discovery of the oldest source might well answer such questions, since it would be closer to Jesus.

The solution accepted today by many NT scholars is the so-called 2-source hypothesis worked out in the 19th century by Karl Lachmann and Hans J. Holtzmann. It was developed into a 4-source hypothesis by Canon Streeter's *The Four Gospels* (1924). Literary analysis and editorial techniques show that Mark was used as a source by Matthew and Luke. A second source may have consisted primarily of sayings of Jesus, since this would ac-

count for the material common to Matthew and
Luke (e. g. Matt. 10:26-33 = Luke 12:2-9; Matt. 5:
3-12 and Luke 6:20-23, etc.). This sayings or logia
source is usually called Q (from German *Quelle*). Its
exact composition and written existence is still under
debate. Finally both Matthew and Luke had separate
sources for their special material. Schematically the
solution can be represented as follows:

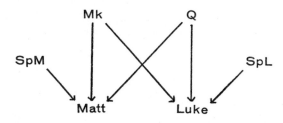

Mk   Q

SpM   SpL

Matt   Luke

     Mark (or, as some supposed, an earlier form
of Mark) and Q were thus the earliest sources.
Matthew and Luke were necessarily later and secondary. (Implications for Matthaean authorship
were variously interpreted.) But this source theory,
important as it is, did not solve the problems of
writing the life of Jesus. Papias had already stated
that Mark was "without order." Wilhelm Wrede
showed that the order in Mark was theological, not
historical, and was due to the author himself. None
of the Gospels were, in the judgment of much critical history, written by an eyewitness; all were com-

posed 35 years and more after the Resurrection and are thus not primary documents.

It is not surprising therefore that the attempts in the 19th century to write the life of Christ in an objective, historicistic fashion were unsuccessful. Albert Schweitzer wrote the history and the obituary of these biographies in *The Quest of the Historical Jesus.* Each scholar produced a Jesus in his own image. Martin Kähler's famous monograph, *Der sogenannte historische Jesus und der geschichtliche, biblische Christus (The So-called Historical Jesus and the Historical, Biblical Christ),* showed that none of these reconstructed, objective Jesus pictures would have called forth the faith of the Christians. Nineteenth-century historicism had erred in not recognizing that the Gospel was a new form in world literature, not biography, but kerygmatic witness to Jesus, that rendered the separation of the historical Jesus from the kerygma impossible. The analysis of synoptic sources was well done. Its validity still stands for many NT scholars despite scattered attacks that attempt to show the priority of Matthew. But it did not lead to the Jesus of history.

B. THE STUDY OF THE ORAL PERIOD

Both Old and New Testament critical studies had thus succeeded in showing the literary and temporal gap between the composition of the Biblical texts and the periods of history they describe. Out of the "failure" of literary criticism was born *Form-*

geschichte (form history, though the usual English translation is form criticism). Form criticism investigates the forms and patterns in ancient literature in order to set them into their place in the history of literature and to determine the cultural or religious setting that originally produced and used the form (Sitz im Leben). It seeks to work back from the text to the setting of the original core of a literary form by defining and removing the later additions, modifications, made in the oral period and by the literary editor who arranged the material into a consecutive literary document. Study of this latter stage is often called *Redaktionsgeschichte*.

1. *Assumptions of Form Criticism*

Form criticism was in use in the study of classical literature and folk literature before it was taken over by Biblical critics. It was primarily the work of H. Gunkel, Albrecht Alt, and other German scholars in the Old Testament, K. L. Schmidt, Martin Dibelius, and Rudolf Bultmann in the New Testament that led to the development of the method. In the Old Testament it was first applied to the Psalter but was later extended to practically every book. In the NT the first generation of scholars (1920–40) concentrated on the Synoptic Gospels. In more recent times, following the lead of Ernst Lohmeyer, more attention has been paid to the epistolary literature and Revelation. Certain general assumptions lie behind the method.

a. The ancient world was bound more by oral

tradition than the modern world and was more faithful in its preservation and transmission.

b. Behind the Biblical documents lie smaller literary units (often called pericopes in NT scholarship) which have their roots in the life of earliest Christianity or in very early Israelite tradition.

c. The literary forms of these smaller units are, in general, shared with the contemporary world, be it the ancient Near East in OT literature or with Judaism and Hellenistic civilization in the NT. These oral forms follow conventions that can be inductively determined from an examination of the material available. They are often conservative in preserving details long after their significance is forgotten. On the other hand, the possibility must not be ruled out that a new and original development may take place in the history of a form (e. g. Albrecht Alt's apodictic form of law; cf. chapter 5 below).

2. Form Criticism of the OT

It would be too much even to list all the forms discovered in the OT. Scholars distinguish between prose and poetic forms. In prose such general categories as speeches, records, laws, and narrative are discussed and subdivided in the Pentateuch. Poetic forms include the song, the hymn, the lament, the thanksgiving, the liturgy, the royal psalm, and the oracle. Wisdom literature has as its basic form the poetical sentence, but this may be expanded into the riddle, the parable, the fable or allegory.

Many of these are widely subdivided, e. g. narratives may be classed as legend (an episode with an historical basis that is intended to instruct or give the origin of a name or a ritual, etc.), myth (legend in a supernatural form, i. e. indicative of direct activity of a god in the affairs of men, not used in a pure form in the OT), autobiographical narrative (written in first person "I" style), annals, court history, etc. It is obvious that categorizations are often also value judgments on the historical value of a particular narrative.

Along with form criticism often goes what has been called tradition history, that is, the connection of certain types of material with a particular place (Abraham with Hebron and Mamre, Gen. 18 and 23; Isaac with Beersheba, Gen. 26, etc.) or a particular theological or historical conception. Thus what Von Rad has called the Creed of Israel in Deut. 26:5 ff. ("A wandering Aramaean was my father," etc.) served as the nucleus around which he sees the Exodus legends gathered in a formula that had its Sitz im Leben in the Festival of Weeks (related to the Canaanite harvest festival, but interpreted from Israel's history). Interpreted in this manner the Pentateuch becomes a great credo, a confession of faith based upon Israel's past. Form criticism and tradition history attempt to show how Israel's history was from its very beginning interpreted through Israel's faith.

The method of OT form criticism can perhaps

be exemplified by the description of how the covenant form of law used in Mesopotamian and Hittite law codes may shed light on the OT. In the ancient Near East the author of a law code is always the sovereign, who makes a unilateral arrangement with his underlings as their suzerain lord. The relationship is spelled out in a formal document to which the vassal swore obedience. The king did not swear, since the vassal had the obligation to trust him. The form can be summarized as follows (according to George Mendenhall): (1) Preamble, giving the author's (ruler's) name and titles. (2) Historical prologue, giving the king's benevolent deeds done in the past in the "I-Thou" form of address. (3) Stipulations, including the ruling out of any foreign relations on the basis of a claim to exclusive overlordship. (4) Provision for deposit in temple and periodic public reading. (5) List of gods who serve as witnesses (cf. adaptation of form in Deut. 32:1, where heaven and earth are called as witnesses, etc.). (6) Blessings-curses formula on the vassals to insure obedience. In the Decalog in Exodus 20 and in the covenant of Joshua 24 this basic form is followed, changed distinctively, however, by the fact that there is no overlord for Israel outside of Jahweh, and the historical prologue is the Exodus. Not all elements listed above are present. Here form criticism shows the distinctive elements in the OT use of this ancient form as well as its Sitz im Leben.

3. *Form Criticism of the New Testament*

Form criticism has been most extensively applied to the synoptic gospels in the NT. K. L.
Schmidt's study of the Gospel of Mark came to the
conclusion that the Gospel was constructed out of
smaller units that existed prior to the Gospel's composition and were placed into order and woven together by the evangelist's notes of time and space.
The Gospel's primary interest was Christological.
Form criticism attempted to classify these earlier
short sections according to form and to determine
the "laws" governing their oral transmission. It
noted that sayings and not sermons were what were
passed on, that Jesus' conversations were normally
presented with only one or two interlocutors, or
with a group of anonymous opponents. It concluded
that the earlier form of a narrative was liable to
be the more simple with elaborations added in
later traditions. Only the Passion and Easter stories
were exceptions to this rule. K. L. Schmidt was
not able by his method to break them down into
smaller, originally unconnected narratives. Yet even
here the narative was interpreted in the light of
Easter by the early church.

The classification of the forms was worked out
by Martin Dibelius and Rudolf Bultmann (whose
terminology is followed here). The material of the
Gospels is divided into two main categories: sayings and narratives. Sayings are subdivided into
apophthegmata (short stories that frame one saying

of Jesus, e. g. Matt. 11:2-9), logia (sayings without any particular historical framework, e. g. wisdom logia as in Matt. 6:34b, apocalyptic logia as in Mark 13:3 ff., or law logia as in Matt. 5:21 f.), and parables.

In all classes critics regard some sayings as authentic and some as creations of the early church. It is not the form but other factors which determine authenticity, since Jesus used *no* new or peculiar literary forms. Narratives are divided into miracle stories, which in form are similar to Jewish and Hellenistic healing stories, and legends. The term legend is not used pejoratively, but descriptively to denote a story intended to be read *(legenda)*. A legend may or may not be historically grounded; in either case, according to the proponents of form criticism, its purpose is to instruct the reader or "glorify the central figure" of the legend. Examples of supposed legends are the confession at Caesarea Philippi (Mark 8:27-33) and most parts of the Passion and Easter narratives. All classifications listed above may be further refined and subdivided.

What are the general conclusions that form critics make? (1) Positively, another tool has been perfected that carries the study of early Christian tradition back a stage behind the earliest documents. Critics claim that they can recover the earliest form by removing later modifications and additions. (2) Martin Dibelius was convinced that the Sitz im Leben of all synoptic materials was the preaching

of the early church ("Am Anfang war die Predigt").
In a sense he was supported by C. H. Dodd's re-
searches into the earliest form of the Christian sermons. Others find the location of early material in
the liturgical or catechetical needs of the early
church. All critics are agreed that form criticism
cannot take the reader back behind the preaching
of the church to earlier objective accounts of Jesus'
life and teaching. (3) Some students of the New
Testament also point out that form criticism need
not lead to historical scepticism. The material recovered is characterized by sobriety of approach, by
a lack of magical enlargement, and by a simplicity
that contrasts strongly with the apocryphal gospels.

Form criticism has not been as readily accepted
in the Anglo-Saxon world as in continental Europe.
It is frequently criticized for having neglected the
effect that the great personalities of the early church
would have had on the tradition, for disregarding the
specific nature of tradition in Judaism (cf. Chapter
4), and for regarding the earliest gospel materials
as belonging in the category of "minor literature."

Form criticism in the other NT literature is still
in its infancy. However, it has already made contributions to our understanding of the early church.
Oscar Cullmann, for example, has isolated the early
creeds in the epistles, that begin with short, one-
clause confessions (e. g. Jesus is Lord, 1 Cor. 12:3).
Much attention has been paid to the isolating of
early hymns which are quoted in the NT (espe-

cially in Pauline literature) — at times to be corrected or interpreted by additions of the Biblical author quoting them, e. g., Phil. 2:6-11; Col. 1:15-20; 1 Tim. 3:16. Many have their origin in the baptismal rites of the early church. These hymns, according to form criticism, give us a glance into the theology of an entirely different strain of early Christianity, called early Christian enthusiasm by some scholars. The isolation of acclamations in the epistles and Revelation (Amen, Abba, cf. Rom. 8:15, and the cries of the heavenly beings in Rev. 4:8, 11, etc.) give us an insight into early liturgical life. The probable borrowing of parenetical and catechetical material from Hellenism (Haustafeln, catalogs of virtues and vices) and Judaism and the setting given to this material in catechetical instruction provides early material for understanding the concern for Christian life in the earliest stages of the church. Much still remains to be done here, but already the importance of worship life in the early church has been made clear, as C. F. D. Moule's *The Birth of the New Testament* has recently shown.

In recent years a new development has taken place. Early form critics disregarded the editorial work of the synoptic authors in compiling, arranging, and narrating their Gospels as later and therefore secondary. Recently interest has shifted to an evaluation of this material as the primary source material for understanding the intention and theology of the Gospels as they now stand. Redaction history, as it is called, regards each Gospel as an important work in its own right. Theologies of Matthew, Mark, and Luke based on their editorial changes have been and are being produced. As a result, NT scholarship today is finding it necessary to rewrite much of the history of early Christianity. (Cf. Chap. 5)

BIBLIOGRAPHY

A. Old Testament Source and Form Criticism

Bentzen, Aage. *Introduction to the Old Testament.* 2d ed. Copenhagen: Gad, 1952.

Childs, Brever. *Memory and Tradition in Israel.* Naperville, Ill.: Alec R. Allenson, 1962.

Eissfeldt, Otto. *Introduction to the Old Testament.* Oxford: Basil Blackwell, 1964.

Koch, Klaus. *The Growth of the Biblical Tradition: The Development of Form Criticism.* New York: Charles Scribner's Sons, 1967.

Mendenhall, George E. *Law and Covenant in Israel and the Ancient Near East.* Pittsburgh: The Biblical Colloquim, 1955.

Noth, Martin. *Überlieferungsgeschichte des Pentateuchs.* 2. Aufl. Stuttgart: W. Kohlhammer Verlag, 1960 (1948).

Ryder, E. T. "Form Criticism of the Old Testament," *Peake's Commentary on the Bible,* edd. Matthew Black and H. H. Rowley. London: Thomas Nelson, 1962. Pp. 91—95 (with a good bibliography).

Weiser, Arthur. *The Old Testament: Its Formation and Development.* New York: Association Press, 1961.

Westermann, Claus. *A Thousand Years and a Day.* Philadelphia: Muhlenberg, 1962.

———. *Grundformen prophetischer Rede.* München: Chr. Kaiser Verlag, 1960.

B. New Testament Source and Form Criticism

Bornkamm, Günther. *Jesus of Nazareth.* Trans. Irene and Fraser McLusky. New York: Harper, 1960. Appendix I, pp. 215—20.

Bultmann, Rudolf. *Die Geschichte der synoptischen Tradition*. 3. Aufl. Göttingen: Vandenhoeck & Ruprecht, 1957. Trans. John Marsh. *The History of the Synoptic Tradition*. New York: Harper & Row, 1963.

Cullmann, Oscar. *The Earliest Christian Confessions*. London: Lutterworth Press, 1953.

————. "The Plurality of the Gospels as a Theological Problem in Antiquity," *The Early Church*. Philadelphia: Westminster Press, 1956. Pp. 37—54.

Dibelius, Martin. *Die Formgeschichte des Evangeliums*. 3. Aufl. Tübingen: J. C. B. Mohr, 1959. Trans. (2d. ed.) as *From Tradition to Gospel: Gospel Criticism and Christology*. New York: Charles Scribner's Sons, 1935 (1964).

Dinkler, E. "Form Criticism of the New Testament," *Peake's Commentary on the Bible*, edd. Matthew Black and H. H. Rowley. London: Thomas Nelson, 1962. Pp. 683—85.

Dodd, C. H. *The Apostolic Preaching and its Developments*. 2nd ed. New York/London: Harper & Brothers, 1951 (1944).

Grant, Frederick C. *The Gospels: Their Origin and Their Growth*. New York: Harper, 1957.

Knox, W. L. *The Sources of the Synoptic Gospels*. Cambridge: University Press, 1953—57.

Moule, C. F. D. *The Birth of the New Testament*. New York: York: Harper & Row, 1962.

Redlich, E. Basil. *Form Criticism*. London: Duckworth, 1939.

Riesenfeld, Harold. *The Gospel Tradition and Its Beginnings*. London: Mowbrays, 1957.

Streeter, Burnett Hillman. *The Four Gospels: A Study of Origins*. 4th impression, revised. London: Macmillan, 1930.

Taylor, Vincent. *The Formation of the Gospel Tradition*. London: Epworth Press, 1933.

Wilder, Amos N. *The Language of the Gospel. Early Christian Rhetoric*. New York: Harper & Row, 1964.

4

The New Quest for the Historical Jesus

For 200 years critical Biblical scholarship sought to describe the historical Jesus whom the Biblical documents contained. The quest ended in a dead-end street. All the literary and historical work, the source analysis, psychological investigation, and form criticism had produced a picture not of the historical Jesus, but of the faith of the early church as proclaimed in the kerygma: Jesus, raised from the dead, is Lord and Messiah. Historical analysis seemed unable to go beyond this kerygmatic theology. Martin Kähler's position, that the faith of the early church was founded upon the Christ as the church preached Him and not upon the Jesus of 19th century historiography, seemed fully justified.

A. BULTMANN ON THE HISTORICAL JESUS

How has recent scholarship reacted to this view? Here, as in many areas of NT scholarship, Rudolf Bultmann's work has been the center around which NT scholarship has ranged itself. Bultmann's answer to the dilemma was to give up entirely the quest for the historical Jesus and to regard the Easter preaching of the early church as determinative for faith; it is the Christ of preaching (i. e. as believed in by the church after Easter), not the Jesus according to the flesh, who is the Lord. The risen Christ is the eschatological event. The historical Jesus is so to speak hidden. We can know nothing of His personality or inner development. All that is important for faith is that Jesus did exist (Rudolf Bultmann's well known "Dasz"). This historical existence prevents the kerygma from being turned into myth, mere religiosity, or mere ethical demands. In that sense Jesus is necessary for the kerygma of the church. Historically, however, His theology is a part of the history of Judaism, a presupposition (Voraussetzung) for NT theology, not a part of it. Faith does not rest upon our knowledge of the historical Jesus, but upon our being confronted by the kerygmatic call to decision of the early Christian proclamation.

On the one hand Rudolf Bultmann felt that he was able to free faith from the results of historical research. *Sola fide* implies a faith that requires no historical substratum or verification. On the other

Biblical Studies Today

hand, Bultmann felt himself free to continue historical investigation of the prekerygma strands of the New Testament. As a historian he could identify material in the Gospels that went authentically back to the historical Jesus without needing to incorporate this understanding into New Testament theology.

Behind this solution lay the understanding of history of existential philosophy. The facts of history are not the whole of history. What is truly "historical" is the interpretation of the facts that confronts me with its demand and call to decision. That interpretation lies in the NT in the post-Easter church.

B. THE NEW QUEST

Bultmann's answer did not prove final. Significantly, it was among his own pupils that the reaction began, though it has spread far beyond the school. In 1953 Ernst Käsemann read a paper entitled "The Problem of the Historical Jesus" to a meeting of old Marburg students. This paper inaugurated the post-Bultmannian "new quest for the historical Jesus" (the phrase is James M. Robinson's).

Ernst Käsemann did not wish to repudiate his teacher entirely but to carry his critical results positively and theologically forward. Käsemann too states that a biography of Jesus' life cannot be written. The Gospels simply do not give us the necessary information. Nor do the *bruta facta*, the bare facts of history, recovered by the techniques of modern historiography, bring us any closer to Jesus. Rather, according to Käsemann, like the writers of the NT itself, who

44

show a noteworthy diversity of understanding and variety of interpretation of the historical facts (to say nothing of their selection and arrangement), we must look for the historical Jesus *in* the kerygma, "for continuity in the historical discontinuity." If we do not discover the continuity that is presupposed in the kerygma, Käsemann feels, then the *extra nos* (objective) dimension of our salvation will be lost and the kerygma and the kerygmatic Christ reduced to mere anthropology. Our faith will only become faith in the church — even if it is the early church. Early Christianity saw a continuity between the historical Jesus and the Christ of faith. Unless we are ready to concede that there is no difference between the Easter faith of the church and mythology and thus become docetic, we must see that this continuity is in reality there. Ernst Käsemann does not attempt to replace the Christ of the kerygma with the historical Jesus (the error of liberalism). Rather, the question about the historical Jesus is legitimately the question for the continuity of the Gospel in the discontinuity of succeeding periods of time and in the variety of expression in the kerygma. So the problem is, how shall we with our critical presuppositions and historical method reach the historical Jesus through the kerygmatic Christ?

This lecture began the new quest. While it originated among the Bultmann students, the quest soon spread across schools of NT research. The post-Bultmannians recognize that modern critical

45

methods make the task of seeking the historical Jesus difficult. Very few facts about the life of Jesus can be known (home in Galilee, death by crucifixion in Jerusalem, etc.). The post-Bultmannians are not interested in extending this list of known facts. They seek rather to identify the authentic words of Jesus in the Gospels, the claim He makes for Himself, and the actions that characterize Him. But authenticity at once implies a criterion, since form criticism has tended to discredit all sayings in the Gospels. According to the post-Bultmannians there are no *formal* criteria for Jesus' words that will distinguish them from the words of other Jews of first century Palestine.

In his first lecture Ernst Käsemann proposed a conceptual criterion. The post-Bultmannians have largely followed him. The criterion is intentionally severe: authentic sayings of Jesus in the Gospels are only those which cannot be placed into the mouth of contemporary Judaism and which cannot be ascribed to the faith or historical circumstances of the post-Easter church. Of course, this criterion does not make clear what united Jesus with Judaism and what He held in immediate continuity with the early church. Käsemann's lecture also gave examples as to how this criterion should be applied to the logia of the Gospels. More important, it brought to the fore the importance and the legitimacy of the quest for the continuity of the Gospel.

C. THE POST-BULTMANNIAN HISTORICAL JESUS

The Bultmann school soon produced two lengthy accounts of Jesus' message and historical position in Günther Bornkamm's *Jesus of Nazareth* (1956) and Hans Conzelmann's article "Jesus Christus" (1959) in the encyclopedia *Die Religion in Geschichte und Gegenwart* and numerous articles on aspects of the search.

The Bultmann school has agreed, in general, that certain aspects of Jesus' teaching were historical. The center of His preaching was the reign of God *(basileia)*. His own works possessed eschatological significance (Matt. 11:12 = Luke 16:16; references are to passages regarded as genuine Jesus logia by various members of the Bultmann school, if not by all). In confronting men Jesus claimed them for the *basileia*. His words and actions revealed a claim *(Anspruch,* i. e. self-understanding) higher than that of the rabbis, for He placed Himself over the Decalog (Matt. 5:21 ff.), the Sabbath (Mark 2:23), and demons (Mark 3:22-27). No rabbi or prophet had ever dared to do this. Jesus may well have regarded Himself as inspired (Käsemann) or have had a sense of great authority (Bornkamm), as His use of "Amen" at the beginning of sentences shows (contrary to where an acclamation ought to be and was normally placed; cf. also Matt. 12:28). "Jesus dared to make God's will as relevant as if He stood in God's place. . . . His manner was that of a man who dared to act in God's stead, in that He . . . drew sinners close to Him, who would have had to flee God without Him" (Ernst Fuchs). "The only category fit to this claim is independent of whether He himself used it and demanded it or not, that category which His disciples used for Him, namely that of the Messiah." (Käsemann)

This last sentence raises a problem. Did Jesus understand Himself as Messiah? (The question is *not* whether the post-Bultmannians believe Jesus is the Messiah!) Here opinions split inside the school. Käsemann, from whom the last quotation stems, answers that it is impossible to give a positive answer. He holds that Jesus did not use the term Son of Man of Himself. All occurrences of the term are due to the theological reflection of the early church. Since the Gospels do not place the terms Lord, Son of God, or Messiah into Jesus' mouth, these terms also are evidence of the Christology and apocalyptic of the post-Easter church. Jesus' authentic words paint no picture of the future. Hans Conzelmann and Philip Vielhauer hold the same view, the latter supporting it with the observation that no passage in the Gospels brings the *basileia* (the heart of Jesus' proclamation) into proximity with the Son of Man concept. Jesus placed His message, not His person, into the center of His proclamation and work.

Another group of post-Bultmannians takes a more positive stand. Bultmann himself had already spoken of a Christology implicit in the words of Jesus and had regarded those Son of Man sayings that referred to the eschatological future as authentic Jesus logia. Günther Bornkamm supports him in this, while Bornkamm's students Heinz Eduard Tödt and Ferdinand Hahn have worked out extensive documentation to support this view. The key passage for them is Mark 8:38, where Jesus distinguishes Himself from the Son of Man — if the passage is taken at face value. What is gained here is a point of historical contact for the extensive creative activity of the post-Easter church, according to this school of thought, which placed so many Son of Man sayings into the mouth of Jesus. (Another Bultmann student, Eduard Schweizer, rejects these sayings entirely, but accepts those that speak of the Son of Man in the present, e. g. Matt. 8:18-22, as genuine.)

An extremely radical group of Bultmann pupils criticizes the entire attempt to reconstruct Jesus' proclamation as basically inconsistent with Bultmann's existential theology. For these critics the proper function of interpretation is to seek the Christian understanding of existence in the historical quest. (Herbert Braun, James M. Robinson)

D. THE CONSERVATIVE POSITION

Ernst Käsemann's lecture excited interest and reaction far beyond the Bultmann school. In the Anglo-Saxon world it intensified research that had never really died down. British scholars have generally shown more scepticism over against the results and values of form criticism (with the exception, perhaps, of Robert H. Lightfoot) and more faith in the historical framework of Mark's Gospel. Vincent Taylor, for example, had been preparing for a life of Christ some years before Käsemann's article appeared. The new quest served to sharpen the differences in approach between British and continental scholars.

Reaction also came within the Roman Catholic Church. Some Roman scholars have attacked the Bultmann school by discrediting form criticism on the basis of a dogmatic understanding of the structure of early church order. If the Twelve served as a church governing body under Peter, we cannot suppose that traditions about Jesus would be passed on without rather strict control. Here the Twelve are used as an external security for the tradition. Other Roman scholars have appealed to the character of the Gospels as Scripture. If the writers were conscious that they were writing Scripture, they would consciously attempt to keep all personally determined material out of the tradition they passed on.

Most Roman Catholic theologians, however, do not attempt to discredit form criticism from such a dogmatic position. They too regard form criticism as an indispensable tool of the interpreter, but attempt to show that there is a sociological continuity between the pre- and post-Easter situation of the disciples (Sitz im Leben); such continuity gives the results of form criticism greater historical value for recovering the historical Jesus than is generally assumed. The disciples had faith before Easter also, even if the content was modified in the post-Easter church. Thus a continuity is secured for the tradition that carries it back prior to the Easter faith of the writers (Schürmann). Basically this argument is based upon the Roman understanding of tradition.

The Protestant conservative reaction has tried to validate the tradition in different fashion. The Uppsala school has tried to show that the concept of oral tradition presupposed in form criticism is not that of NT Judaism or the NT. In 1957 Harold Riesenfeld (*The Gospel Tradition and Its Beginnings*) suggested that Jesus should be regarded as a rabbinic teacher, not primarily as a preacher. This means that tradition (*paradosis*), not preaching (kerygma) is the true Sitz im Leben for the Gospel tradition. Jewish rabbis made their pupils learn their teaching by heart, as *Pirke Avoth*, other tractates of the Mishnah, and still later Jewish documents show. One must presuppose that the same rabbinical methods were current in Jesus' day. (Riesenfeld's student Birger Gerhardson attempted to document this assertion in a massive dissertation.) If Riesenfeld is correct, then the tradition behind Jesus' words, at least, goes back directly to Jesus Himself. The Synoptics present His exoteric [sic], public teaching, while the Johannine tradition contains His esoteric interpretation of His work given to His disciples. In this way Riesenfeld tries to regain the *ipsissima verba* of Jesus. The necessity of projecting rabbinic methods of a later age back into the time of Jesus, as Riesen-

feld's critics have been quick to point out, is a weak
point in his approach.

Joachim Jeremias represents a second "conservative" reaction to the post-Bultmannian attempt to
reconstruct the historical Jesus. According to Jeremias the Bultmannians are in danger of reducing
Jesus to a mere Christ idea, a docetic symbol, and
thus destroying the reality of God's action in the
man Jesus. Jeremias is concerned to find the actual
words of Jesus that lie behind the Gospels. Kerygma
itself as he sees it demands this historical research.
Today the scholar has the means to achieve this
goal in his use of source analysis, form criticism,
tradition history, his knowledge of contemporary
Judaism, his knowledge of the Aramaic language of
Jesus' day, and in the recovery of the eschatological
character of Jesus' teaching and work. We are no
longer in danger of modernizing Jesus in our own
image. By careful historical research, Jeremias main-
tains, we can recover the *ipsissima vox* of Jesus and
thus be placed before God Himself. It is the words
of Jesus that are the call *(Ruf)* to which the kerygma
of the church is only response *(Antwort)*. Jesus' call
is the revelation to which the kerygma is the witness.

The Bultmannians criticize both Riesenfeld and
Jeremias. The conservative attempt to validate the
message of Jesus is, in effect, a reduction, if not
destruction, of the *sola Scriptura* principle of Reformation theology, the Bultmannians contend. For
Jeremias only the *verba ipsissima* of Jesus are the

true Scriptures. Both Riesenfeld and Jeremias make history the norm of Scripture; in effect, say their critics, this is still the error of older liberal historicism which destroys the Reformation dialectic of Word of God and Scriptures. Thus the lines are drawn along hermeneutical lines.

E. RESULTS AND PROBLEMS

In outline the New Quest can be summarized briefly.

1. It is generally agreed that the historical Jesus is necessary to guard against a docetic reduction of the human Jesus and the NT Gospel to a depersonalized ethical myth. Bultmann's "Dasz" is not enough. (The radical wing of the Bultmann school contests this.)

2. An objective biography of Jesus is impossible and undesirable. We know Jesus only in the interpretation given Him in the Scriptures.

3. There is therefore a continuity within the discontinuity. Good Friday and Easter together form the decisive event. It is the Lord and Messiah of Easter (Acts 2:36) in whom we believe and whom we proclaim.

BIBLIOGRAPHY

Althaus, Paul. *Fact and Faith in the Kerygma of Today.* Philadelphia: Muhlenberg, 1959. British title: *The So-Called Kerygma and the Historical Jesus.*

Bornkamm, Günther. *Jesus of Nazareth.* New York: Harper, 1960

Braaten, Carl E. and Roy A. Harrisville, edd. *The Historical Jesus and the Kerygmatic Christ. Essays on the New Quest of the Historical Jesus.* New York: Abingdon, 1964.

Biblical Studies Today

Bultmann, Rudolf. *Das Verhältnis des urchristlichen Christus Botschaft zum historischen Jesus.* 3. Aufl. Heidelberg: Carl Winter, 1962. (English translation in Braaten-Harrisville, above.)

Conzelmann, Hans. "Jesus Christus," *Die Religion in Geschichte und Gegenwart.* 3. Aufl. Tübingen: J. C. B. Mohr, 1959. III, cols. 619—53.

Frör, Kurt. *Biblische Hermeneutik.* München: Chr. Kaiser Verlag, 1961. Pp. 260—77.

Jeremias, Joachim. *Das Problem des historischen Jesus.* Stuttgart: Calwer Verlag, 1960. Trans. as *The Problem of the Historical Jesus.* Philadelphia: Fortress Press, 1964.

Kähler, Martin. *Der sogenannte historische Jesus und der geschichtliche, biblische Christus.* 2. Aufl. München: Chr. Kaiser Verlag, 1961. Trans. into English with intro. by Carl Braaten: *The So-called Historical Jesus and the Historic, Biblical Christ.* Philadelphia: Fortress Press, 1964.

Käsemann, Ernst. "Das Problem des historischen Jesus," *Zeitschrift für Theologie und Kirche,* LI (1954), 125—53. Reprinted in *Exegetische Versuche und Besinnungen,* I. Göttingen: Vandenhoeck & Ruprecht, 1960. Pp. 187—213. Trans. W. J. Montague, *Essays on New Testament Themes.* Naperville, Ill.: Alec R. Allenson, 1964. Pp. 15—47.

Ristow, H. and K. Matthiae, edd. *Der historische Jesus und der kerygmatische Christus.* Berlin: Evangelische Verlagsanstalt, 1961.

Robinson, James M. *A New Quest of the Historical Jesus.* Naperville, Ill.: Alec R. Allenson, 1959.

Schweitzer, Albert. *The Quest of the Historical Jesus.* New York: Macmillan, 1910.

Stauffer, Ethelbert. *Jesus and His Story.* Trans. Richard and Clara Winston. New York: Knopf, 1960.

Zahrndt, Heinz. *Es begann mit Jesus von Nazareth.* Gütersloh: Gütersloher Verlagshaus Gerd Mohn, 1960. Trans. J. S. Bowden, *The Historical Jesus.* New York: Harper, 1963.

5

The Bible in the World of Its Day

Religionsgeschichte and
Biblical Records

The Bible came into a world already burdened with religious history and spoke to that world. Only in the context of that world can the distinctive and original elements of the Biblical message be isolated and understood. To give the Bible a spurious originality by treating it as historically unique in every aspect is to run the risk of not understanding the meaning God placed into it. Biblical authors used languages whose vocabulary already had religious, social, legal, political, and philosophical denotations and connotations. Their literary forms were sometimes adapted from surrounding peoples, who had developed the forms in both their secular and religious life. Forms of worship existed before the Jewish temple liturgy was initiated.

The historical approach to the Bible attempts in the first place to determine the extent of this cultural borrowing and to use that knowledge as a tool of interpretation. Scholars ask what literary forms and content, mythical expressions, literary conventions, etc. came from the surrounding world. In the second place, critical historical scholarship asks what changes occurred in the material borrowed. How did the basic and essential content of Israel's faith or the Easter faith correct, modify, or refute borrowed thoughts and forms even as they were used? In other words, scholarship attempts to determine that which unites the Bible with the religious world about it and that which is peculiar to and original in the Bible. The following paragraphs give just a few examples of research on a multidirectional front.

A. THE OLD TESTAMENT WORLD

As the crossroads of the ancient Near East, Palestine was naturally brought into contact with Egypt, Syria, Eastern Asia Minor, Persia, and Mesopotamia — Old Testament specialists maintain. In the OT period Sumerian, Ugaritic, Egyptian, Akkadian, Aegean, Babylonian, Persian, and Greek culture and religion all at one time or another influenced Palestine, to say nothing of its own native Canaanite religion. Anyone who has read Is. 44–46 knows how real and close this world was to Israel. The scholar knows that a phenomenological approach to the OT cannot explain everything in it. Only Israelites and

Greeks of all ancient peoples began to write history rather than annals (the mere listing of events) — and that quite independently of each other. Here it is clear that the "Creed" of Israel, as described in Chapter 3, was of decisive influence in the writing of history. It was this very credo which allowed Israel to lay surrounding cultures under contribution, without thereby losing her own individuality and uniqueness. Revelation did not mean exclusive separation.

1. *Influence in Form*

Scholars claim that various psalm forms were common to Israel and surrounding cultures. The parallel between Ps. 104 and the earlier Hymn of Pharoah Akhnaton of Egypt has often been used to show that direct literary influence is probable. Other suggestions have been made. Israel probably borrowed both the form of Wisdom Literature as well as the institution of the professional class of "wise man" from Egypt and the ancient world. Prov. 22: 17—23:12, for example, borrows content and form from the proverbs of Amen-en-opet of Egypt. The Pentateuch borrowed the form of casuistic law and the covenant treaty form from ancient Hittite culture, while Mari already knew the messenger oracle form found in the prophets.

2. *Influence in Content*

The use of historical methodology has also led experts to posit the influence of ancient Near Eastern myth and religion in the content of the OT. It is argued, for example, that the Canaanitic and Babylonian creation myth echoes in places in the OT, e. g. in Ps. 74:12-14 and Hab. 3. In this myth creation is the result of a struggle between the forces of good and evil, the evil dragon (Leviathan) being defeated. The dragon's body (Tiamat in Babylon) then serves as the material for the creation of the world (cf. Is. 51:9 f.; Ps. 89:10 ff.). The evil=dragon motif recurs in the Apocalypse, as it had earlier. Here, as generally in the OT, a process of historicizing has taken place, that is, mythical language is taken over and related to definite historical events to describe the (present) superiority of Jahweh over all other gods. Jahweh, for example, is called "Rider of clouds," a title used in Canaanite mythology.

Some scholars posit a similar process in the use of the idea of the heavenly council that was prevalent in polytheistic antiquity. The gods meet in council with El at their head, where they serve as the heavenly court (cf. Ps. 89:6 ff.; Job 1:6; 2:1). The heavenly council meets in the OT too, but with a decided difference. This modern view holds that Ps. 82 is the clearest OT example. Here Jahweh calls the gods to task for failing in their appointed mission and threatens them with destruction. No longer is it a council of equals. Though the gods are not denied existence, their subservience to Jahweh is clear. The OT uses all the language of the world about it (hosts, sons of god, angels, etc.) to describe these beings in order to show that there is no god beside Jahweh. Some OT scholars state that it is only in the light of such a background that the prophet Micaiah's description of God in 1 Kings 22:19 and the invitation to praise God in Ps. 148 become clear.

3. *Cultic Influence*

There is much less agreement among OT scholars as to the nature and extent of influence on Israel's cult. Sigmund Mowinckel first suggested, on the basis of the annual enthronement of Marduk in Babylon, that the Festival of Booths served in Israel as the annual enthronement festival of Jahweh at the New Year. On that day the Israelite king was "enthroned" as God's representative with the annual renewal of the covenant and law. This thesis was rejected by Albrecht Alt, who found the Sitz im Leben for the Law in Israel to be the recitation of the Law at each Sabbatical year (based on Deut. 27 and 31:19 ff.); Mowinckel's thesis was by no means buried by this rejection. In this connection Alt made his original contribution to the form critical study of OT law in the distinction between casuistic (represented by the formula "If a man + wrong, then he shall + punishment") and apodictic law (categorical prohibition in second person singular as in the Decalog).

Many Scandinavian and English scholars lay emphasis on the cultic-mythological scheme of the ancient Near East, where the cycle of nature is represented in the myth of the dying and rising god. According to these scholars Israel shared this general mythology until the work of the great eighth century prophets called it into question. But one thing remained: the central importance of the king in cultic observance. He incorporated in his person the representation of the people he ruled before God and the God whom he represented before the people (corporate personality). Ritually he incorporated the fertility process in the New Year's festival, where he became the agent through whom God works life and fertility in nature by annually enacting death and rebirth.

This theory of divine kingship, promoted by S. Hooke, I. Egnell, and A. Bentzen, has broad implications for the understanding of the OT. Certain psalms receive their Sitz im Leben in this annual festival (8, 46, 47, 93, 96-99). The psalms of lamentation, e. g., Ps. 22, apply to the "dying king" on New Year's day. Some even understand Is. 53 within this framework. Other scholars have protested vigorously against this mythicizing of the OT and call for a stronger continuation of Alt's line of research.

Similar questions are raised in regard to the externals of Jewish religion. What was the ikonography of the cherubim? Was there anything distinctive about the form of the temple? Were the sacrificial methods and system of Israel externally different from those of surrounding nations? Essentially, the problem is one of hermeneutics, that is, of the proper method of interpreting the old testament.

B. THE NEW TESTAMENT IN ITS WORLD

The NT originated in a world where many forms of religion were competing for the hearts of men. Judaism, Eastern religions, Greek mysteries, philosophic religion and scepticism, and magic and astrology all crisscrossed the ancient world. The NT, a Greek book, is based upon the history of Jesus, who lived in Aramaic, namely, Semitic, Palestine. With that statement a major problem for New Testament studies is stated, no matter what method of study is used. Against which religious background is one to read the various authors of the NT? This can, perhaps, be made clear by an example. Although many of the NT books were written by men of Palestinian background, their writers often cite from the Septuagint or Greek translation of the OT, even when its text differs from the Hebrew. How then are we to evaluate this fact? Is it valid to judge their use of the OT by the rabbinic or Qumran hermeneutical methods? Should one rather study Hellenistic Judaism? Or should one place himself in the position of the non-Jewish reader and disregard this Jewish background in favor of a Hellenistic approach?

1. *Judaica and the NT*

One set of problems is raised by the study of Judaism and the New Testament. The scholars of the 20s concentrated especially upon rabbinic Ju-

daism of the age of the Tannaim (i. e. down to ca.
A. D. 300). Gustav Dalman, Adolf Schlatter, and
above all, Paul Billerbeck with his massive compila-
tion of materials have enriched NT studies with an
appreciation of rabbinical attitudes toward the Torah,
messianism, eschatology, and literary form. In more
modern times this inquiry has been continued by
J. Jeremias, O. Michel, and W. D. Davies, together
with several notable Jewish scholars (D. Daube, H.
J. Schoeps). This material, however, presents chronological difficulties. None of the written sources go
back to a date prior to approximately A. D. 200.
Many writers have suggested that it is dangerous
to project into early first century Palestine later
attitudes and beliefs.

A second and fruitful area of research has been
in the area of Jewish apocalyptic literature. This
has helped to shed light not only on the language
and form of the Book of Revelation, but also upon
such concepts as "Son of Man" and "kingdom of
God." It was this literature that enabled Johannes
Weiss to show that liberalism was wrong in concen-
trating primarily upon Jesus as an ethical teacher.

The discovery of the Dead Sea Scrolls in 1947 ff.
has contributed immensely to our knowledge of first
century Judaism and the NT. The scrolls show how
fragmentary our knowledge of Judaism in this period
was (and perhaps still is) and prevent us from
making overly broad generalizations. This apocalyptic Essene (as generally agreed) group has so much

similarity to early Christianity that the question of the position of early Christianity inside of Judaism was raised anew (echoes of Renan's famous assertion of a century ago that Christianity was just an Essenism that succeeded were heard from such popular writers as Edmund Wilson and certain incautious scholars.) Just a mere listing of some facts illustrates the complexity.

The Qumran community regarded itself as the true Israel of the last age, the true fulfillment of OT prophecy. It looked forward to messianic deliverers, a Moseslike prophet (cf. Deut. 18:18), a messiah from the line of Aaron (cf. John the Baptist), and a messiah of Israel, i. e. from the line of David. It looked forward to a great eschatological war in the future (cf. Revelation). Its community was bound together by a communal meal and ritual washings. In its organization it was led by a body of twelve and an overseer. Its possessions were held in common. Its literature makes use of forms similar to the NT (hymns, apocalyptic, OT interpretation). Its apocalyptic language has many points of contact with Paul and John, to say nothing of the Apocalypse. The Scrolls' dualistic language reminds many of John's Gospel (light/darkness, truth/error, spirit/flesh, love/hate, death/life), so that the problem of Johannine theology is opened again.

Many scholars think that John the Baptist may have had points of contact with this group, while a few see direct influence upon the early church through the Hellenists or Hebraists of Acts 6—7. Of course, differences are noted and emphasized. The exclusive character of Qumran, for example, contrasts sharply with the missionary thrust of the church.

Hellenistic Judaism, as represented by Philo, Aristeas, IV Maccabees, the Wisdom of Solomon, and Aristobulus, is the third strand of Judaism taken into account by NT scholars. Here Judaism entered into dialog with pagan thought while at the same time borrowing from it. Its use of philosophic categories (logos, wisdom, virtue) as well as its apologetic tone (at times severe, at times conciliatory), presented early Christianity with valuable material (cf. Paul's arguments against the pagans in Romans 1).

2. *Hellenistic Religions and the NT*

There is little controversy today over the relation of the mystery religions, the emperor cult, or Hellenistic philosophy to the NT. It is taken for granted by many scholars that all of them contributed on occasion to the language and conceptual world of Paul, Luke, and the writers of Hebrews and other NT books. Second Peter, for example, shows an acquaintance with the language of the Greek mysteries, while Paul's sermon in Acts 17 cannot be fully appreciated without some knowledge of Hellenistic philosophy.

The major area of conflict and research in Hellenistic religions lies in supposed gnostic influences in the NT. Basing his theory on the work of the *religionsgeschichtliche Schule* (the History of Religions School), Rudolf Bultmann constructed a full-blown "Redeemed redeemer" myth, which he found in Mandaean literature. By supposing that the entire myth was extant when earlier literature used language that suggested the later myth, he posited a pre-Christian origin for the myth upon the basis of Jewish wisdom literature, the Odes of Solomon, the apocryphal acts of the apostles, and the NT itself.

This myth can be summarized as follows. A divine being is sent down from the world of light to our world that is ruled by demonic powers. He is to gather those portions of light that fell from heavenly bliss and were banned to human bodies of flesh. He takes human form himself and reveals himself in his sermons ("I am the way," etc.). Those who have the divine spark recognize him and so come to know themselves and follow him in his return to heaven. Since the particles of light are really a part of the godhead itself, the redeemer really redeems himself. Bultmann's reconstruction has recently been put into question by two incisive critiques written by C. Colpe and H. M. Schenke. These have made a reevaluation of much earlier work by his students necessary, for example, of the "body of Christ" concept in Ephesians.

3. *Examples from the NT*

There is no agreement as to how much the NT is supposed to have borrowed in language and thought from this world. Almost every conclusion of former scholars stands under question today. On the one hand scholars seem generally agreed that some NT language can only be explained by recourse to OT and Jewish thought, e. g., the word *doxa* (glory). Other motifs seem to have developed in the general framework of gnostic language. This is especially true of the theology of the hymns identified by form critics as coming from the early Hellenistic (Greek speaking former pagan) church (Col. 1:15-20 and Eph. 1:5 ff.). (Schille, Käsemann) These hymns are frequently interpreted and corrected theologically even as they are cited. The problem comes when one studies individual concepts, e. g., the "body of Christ" concept in Ephesians (Schlier), in a phenomenological fashion. Is Adam interpreted in a gnostic sense in Rom. 5:12-21, when his sin brings death on all men? How is the idea of "fullness" in Colossians to be interpreted? Others find that the major opponents of Paul in Galatia, Corinth, Philippi, etc., were gnosticizing Christians.

Another example might well be the term *kyrios* (lord) as applied to Christ. Does Lord have the flavor of Jahweh when applied to Christ (i. e., is it primarily an assertion of his godhead?) or is Lord a reflection of the Hellenistic enthronement scheme (cf. e. g. Phil. 2:9-11) where the enthronement of the ruler is followed by his proclamation as lord and the acclamation of those powers who are under him (i. e., does it proclaim his Lordship over the world and all demonic forces in it?) If this problem is generalized, it can be stated as follows: Is the NT to be understood in the sense that the original (Hellenistic) hearers would have understood it (every lexicon has this as a principle) or from the sense that the writer intended to convey (even if his words perhaps do not make it clear)?

The examples given above are intended to show the type of question being debated today. In general, no one is using such materials simply to undermine the uniqueness of Christ, but rather to set into prominence just what it is that is stated about Christ in the NT that is unique. The problem is once again essentially one of hermeneutics, i. e., of the presuppositions and criteria of interpretation. That the NT has to be read as part of a wider world of thought is evident. The problem is, in what direction shall we cast our glance when we lift our eyes from the pages of the NT itself, toward Palestinian Judaism, Hellenistic paganism, both, or neither?

BIBLIOGRAPHY

1. OT

Kraus, Hans-Joachim, "Der gegenwärtige Stand der Forschung am alten Testament," *Die Freiheit des Evangeliums und die Ordnung der Gesellschaft.* München: Chr. Kaiser Verlag, 1952. Pp. 103—32.

Weiser, Arthur. *The Old Testament: Its Formation and Development.* NY: Association Press, 1961. Cf. ch. 3.

Wright, G. Ernest. *The Old Testament Against Its Environment.* London: SCM Press, 1950.

2. NT

Black, Matthew. *The Scrolls and Christian Origins*. London and New York: Thos. Nelson and Sons, Ltd., 1961.

Colpe, Carsten. *Die religionsgeschichtliche Schule*. Göttingen: Vandenhoeck & Ruprecht, 1961.

Cross, Frank More, Jr. *The Ancient Library of Qumran and Modern Biblical Studies*. Garden City, N. Y.: Doubleday & Co., 1958. (Since published as a paperback.)

Grant, Frederick C. *Ancient Judaism and the New Testament*. New York: Macmillan, 1959.

————. *Roman Hellenism and the New Testament*. New York: Scribner, 1962.

Manson, T. W. *The Servant-Messiah*. Cambridge: University Press, 1953.

Stendahl, Krister, ed. *The Scrolls and the New Testament*. New York: Harper, c. 1957.

6

Historical and Hermeneutical Issues in Current Biblical Studies

The previous chapters have described a number of problem areas that are currently under discussion in Biblical studies. The present chapter aims to list others that cannot receive discussion here. Only a general indication of the nature of the problems can be sketched.

A. HISTORICAL QUESTIONS

1. The first issue to be taken up is that of pseudonymity. This is an issue between historical critics of the middle or more extreme positions and representatives of conservative Biblical scholarship. Conservative scholars such as Donald Guthrie will often rule out the possibility of pseudonymous writing in the New Testament with the argument that the obligation to be truthful for a NT author pre-

cludes the possibility of pseudonymity. (Similar arguments are raised in the OT.) The Holy Ghost would not use an essentially deceitful method.

Historical criticism counters this objection with a number of observations. (1) It cannot be gainsaid that the practice was current in Hellenistic, Jewish (Wisdom of Solomon), and later Christian literature (Preaching of Peter, Apocalypse of Peter, etc.). The NT betrays a knowledge of it in 2 Thess. 2:2 and 3:17. (2) One must recognize that pseudonymity existed in different forms, levels, and intentions in antiquity. Apostolic had a different meaning in early Christianity than "written by an apostle." Often it meant the proclamation given under the influence of the Holy Spirit (cf. Paul's opponents in 2 Cor. 10–13). One cannot therefore raise *eo ipso* the accusation of intention to deceive in the case of a pseudonymous work. (3) Some have urged the ancient concept of the name or corporate personality to show how a later pupil might in his master's name meet a new problem with an answer based upon his master's teaching. In this way much of NT scholarship regards Ephesians, the Pastorals, 2 Peter, and possibly Colossians and 2 Thessalonians as pseudonymous works.

2. The nature of Acts is another area that is currently under discussion. Current NT historical scholarship is agreed that Luke has placed a definite theological pattern and concern on his presentation of early Christian history. Scholarship splits rather

sharply on the effect this has had on the historical value of Acts for the writing of early Christian history. German scholarship has tended in recent years to emphasize Luke's theology at the expense of the historical value of Acts. Luke is portrayed as giving an idealized portrait of the early church that is to serve as the model for later periods (Haenchen). Some German critics maintain, for example, that for Luke only the Twelve are apostles, Paul is not (cf. G. Klein). In contrast to Paul, Luke emphasizes the value of natural theology (Vielhauer). With his emphasis on the apostles and the church as the guarantor of orthodoxy Luke stands on the threshold of early Catholicism (see below).

Anglo-Saxon scholars share the view that Luke must be read as theologian as much as historian. They agree that Luke has subjected his sources to a periodization, that he was seeking a theological solution to the delay of the *parousia,* and that his theology is expressed primarily in his selection of material, in his editorial connectives, and above all in the speeches of Acts, which they too regard generally as free compositions in the manner of ancient historiography. But they are at the same time more inclined to find earlier sources and traditions in Acts that can aid in a reconstruction of the history of the early church. W. D. Davies would stand as a typical example of this trend. He finds a Jerusalem source in Acts 1–5 (outside of the speeches of course), an Antioch source in most of chapters 6–15, and a Caesarean or Jerusalem source in 9:31—11:18 and 12. Anglo-Saxon scholars are less inclined to view Luke's theology and historical veracity as mutually exclusive.

3. A third area of current historical research is concerned with describing the number of forms of early Christianity that appear in the NT. One obligation of scholarship is to write the history of the first century of the Christian church. Since Walter Bauer published his *Rechtgläubigkeit und Ketzerei* . . . in 1934, critical scholarship has no longer thought (if it did prior to that) of the history of early Christianity as a falling away from an originally pristine doctrine. Rather the NT is regarded as a document which reveals the unfolding of the faith of the church in the risen Christ through crises that called for ongoing theological debate and doctrinal refinement. It is customary today to speak of particularistic Judaic Christianity, of a more free Hellenistic-Jewish Christianity, of an enthusiastic (or gnostic [Schmithals] or Hellenistic) Christianity, of Pauline Christianity, and of early catholicism (the claim that there is in books of the NT a trend toward a hierarchical clergy, a sacramental system under its control, etc., as in 2 Peter. The term early catholicism is a translation of the German word *Frühkatholizismus.*) The history of the earliest period is derived by critical scholarship from notices in the Pauline corpus and some material from Acts.

The new dimension in the writing of this history

today lies in the place given to early catholicism. Prior to the post-World War II period early catholicism was generally regarded as a later, second century aberration of NT Christianity. Today some scholars find the beginnings of early catholicism in the NT itself, notably in Acts, the Pastorals, 2 Peter (most definitely) and, in some quarters, in Ephesians. John, by way of contrast, is regarded as a fighter against early catholicism. The marks of this early catholicism are a search for authority outside of the kerygma, i. e. in an apostolic authority coupled with a domesticizing of Paul (Luke never calls him an apostle), a recognition of an incipient NT canon, a loss of early Christian eschatological hope leading to a regularization of the clergy and an ascription of authority to the organizational church. One is in Christ so long as he is in the church. It is unlikely that any consensus will be reached in the question of early catholicism in the NT for many years. (Without describing it, one can also mention that a similar controversy is going on in regard to the nature and influence of early Christian enthusiasm.)

B. THEOLOGICAL-HERMENEUTICAL ISSUE

The rise of historical criticism has also raised severe theological problems in Biblical scholarship. Many of these are also hermeneutical problems. A number of these will be mentioned here.

1. Recently a young Scotch theologian now in the United States, James Barr, drastically criticized

the method of linguistic research used in the so-called *Begriffsforschung*, the investigation of the theology contained in a word or group of words. This is the method which lies behind Kittel's *Theologisches Wörterbuch*, the greatest single product of the awakening of theological exegesis and Biblical theology in the 20s of this century. Barr's critique attacks many works in recent Biblical research on a very basic level; it centers on their linguistic methodology in dealing with words as though some sort of abstract general concept existed for the word in isolation. Based on current structural linguistics, this attack is not sympathetic to the current philosophy of language and meaning that predominates in much of continental Europe. Barr also questions the sharp distinction made between Hebrew and Greek thought patterns. This discussion has just begun; the publication of Barr's *Semantics of Biblical Language* in German is bringing the discussion to the fore in continental theology.

2. Even more basic to all branches of theology is the current discussion about Biblical theology. This discussion can be summarized by presenting the problems in a number of questions. Is Biblical theology, so far as the church is concerned, to be a descriptive or a normative discipline? If normative, how does it relate to dogmatics? Is it possible to speak of a Biblical theology at all in critical scholarship, when that scholarship has, in its opinion, radically separated the two testaments? Is it possible,

they say, to speak of a Biblical theology when scholarship has distinguished the theologies of various authors in the Bible (e. g., Isaiah, Paul, author of
Hebrews, Luke) and emphasized the difference in
viewpoint among them? In view of this is it possible
to speak of a Biblical theology when criticism has
raised the question of the canon anew in modern
times? Can one speak of a NT *theology,* since theology by definition implies Biblical truth confronting philosophic thought?

3. This series of questions about Biblical theology makes it clear why two problems in particular
are under discussion in current literature. The first
is the problem of *Heilsgeschichte,* "salvation history"
as it is commonly translated. According to it, the
faith of the Bible is that the triune God in His
creative activity has been active in and through
history to save. This understanding of history has
been called into question by the Enlightenment, by
historical romanticism and idealism, and in modern
times by existential theology. Various attempts have
been made to overcome the difficulty raised by modern historical views. Some have spoken of typology
as the answer to this problem, others of the fact
that all Biblical history lies *sub contrario,* that only
faith can see the once-and-for-all character of history
in Christ. Some have objected that history need
not be defined only in terms of the visible and verifiable. Existential theology has attempted to solve
the problem by making "history" serve primarily as

the ground for a call to personal decision in the here and now, thus, at least in part, it demythologizes Biblical history (making the supernatural elements dispensable). It is only in this wider framework that the demythologizing debate is currently being carried on. The question to be addressed to the above is: Can theology be disinterested in historical facts? Is not the heilsgeschichtliche interpretation itself a fact of Biblical history?

4. This places us before the second and most important problem being discussed today. What is the center of the Scriptures that determines our preunderstanding of it (Vorverständnis) and the questions that we will address to it? This question was raised both by Karl Barth's *Commentary on Romans* and by Rudolf Bultmann's raising of the problem of demythologization. Here too various answers are given today. In the post-Bultmann period some are speaking of the proper question as that which asks for the self-understanding of man. Only this is constant in the NT, while all else is variable. Jesus' call is to faith. In old dogmatic terminology, some scholars contend that the *fides qua* is all important, the *fides quae* is completely variable in the NT! One studies the NT only to bring oneself into question.

Following the Reformation, others seek the center of the NT in the doctrine of justification. Even in the Bultmann school Bultmann is attacked for having discussed Pauline theology primarily as

anthropology in his *Theology of the New Testament*.
Such an approach, it is maintained, undervalues the
place of eschatology in the New Testament and
places Christology, the center, in the wrong position.
The large majority of texts in the NT are not to be
understood existentially but from a different perspective. Ultimately justification and Christology in the
light of eschatology are the center of the NT and
run throughout the NT. Without these the *extra nos*
objective character of NT thought disappears.

BIBLIOGRAPHY

Barr, James. *The Semantics of Biblical Language*. London: Oxford University Press, 1961.

——. "Revelation through History in the Old Testament and in
Modern Theology," *New Theology No. 1*. Edd. Martin E.
Marty and Dean Peerman. New York: Macmillan, 1964.

Bauer, Walter. *Rechtgläubigkeit und Ketzerei im ältesten Chris-
tentum*. 2. Aufl. Tübingen: J. C. B. Mohr, 1964.

Braaten, Carl E. *History and Hermeneutics: New Directions in
Theology Today*, vol. D. Philadelphia: Westminster Press,
1966.

Ebeling, G. "The Meaning of 'Biblical Theology,'" *Word and
Faith*. Philadelphia: Fortress, 1964. Pp. 79—97.

Fuchs, Ernst. *Hermeneutik*. 2. Aufl. Bad Cannstatt: R. Müllerschen
Verlag, 1958.

Pannenberg, Wolfhart, ed. *Offenbarung als Geschichte*. 2. Aufl.
Göttingen: Vandenhoeck & Ruprecht, 1963.

Rust, Eric C. *Salvation History: A Biblical Interpretation*. Rich-
mond, Va.: John Knox Press, 1963.

Robinson, James M. "Basic Shifts in German Theology," *Interpretation*, XVI (1962), 76—97.

Robinson, James McConkey, and John Cobb, edd. *The New Hermeneutic.* New York: Harper & Row, 1964.

Schlatter, Adolf. *Die Theologie des neuen Testaments und die Dogmatik.* Gütersloh: C. Bertelsmann Verlag, 1909.

Schnackenburg, R. *New Testament Theology Today.* New York: Herder and Herder, 1963.

Westermann, Claus, ed. *Essays on Old Testament Interpretation.* London: SCM Press, 1963.

Conclusion

This survey has mentioned only the most discussed views in Biblical scholarship in recent years.
It has left to one side all research that deals with
textual criticism, archaeology and the OT, the languages of the Bible, and the problem of the canon
within the canon. It has not attempted to give any
sort of a report on the present attitude toward specific questions: the authorship of the Pastorals, the
literary genre of Job and Jonah, and a host of similar
questions. Partition theories in 2 Corinthians and
other books have not been mentioned.

Limitations of space have prevented the author's
own evaluations and opinions from intruding themselves. This has been intended as a report and not
as a critique or a presentation of personal views and
positions. Nonetheless, perhaps one or two general
concluding remarks can be included here.

1. There is little doubt that the questions raised
by Rudolf Bultmann have dominated most NT research in recent years. No one person has so determined OT studies in recent years.

2. In spite of Bultmann's dominance, his school
can scarcely be said to have held together. Bultmann pupils now hold widely disparate views on the
historical Jesus, existential interpretation, and the
whole question of hermeneutics.

3. In Germany at least form criticism and demythologizing are no longer burning issues of discussion. Form criticism has established itself as a tool that scholars of every stripe use. Demythologizing has been absorbed into the larger discussion of hermeneutics.

4. Much energy will be expended in writing the history of the OT and NT periods on the basis of the results of form, tradition, and redaction criticism (or history, as the Germans say).

DATE DUE

MAY 15 '87			
MAY 31 '87			
MAR 11 '68			
APR 1 5 1986			
GAYLORD			PRINTED IN U.S A.